Key Element Guide
Continual Service
Improvement

London: TSO

⊠ TSO

information & publishing solutions

Published by TSO (The Stationery Office)
and available from:

Online
www.tsoshop.co.uk

Mail, Telephone, Fax & E-mail
TSO
PO Box 29, Norwich NR3 1GN
Telephone orders/General enquiries:
0870 600 5522
Fax orders: 0870 600 5533
E-mail: customer.services@tso.co.uk
Textphone: 0870 240 3701

TSO Shops
16 Arthur Street, Belfast BT1 4GD
028 9023 8451 Fax 028 9023 5401
71 Lothian Road, Edinburgh EH3 9AZ
0870 606 5566 Fax 0870 606 5588

TSO@Blackwell and other Accredited Agents

Published with the permission of the Office of
Government Commerce on behalf of the Controller
of Her Majesty's Stationery Office

First published 2008

ISBN 9780113310746 (Sold in a pack of 10 copies)
ISBN 9780113311224 (Single copy ISBN)

Printed in the United Kingdom for The Stationery
Office
N5745183   03/08

Contents

Acknowledgements

ITIL AUTHORING TEAM

- Sharon Taylor (Aspect Group Inc) Chief Architect
- Gary Case (Pink Elephant) Author
- George Spalding (Pink Elephant) Author
- Pierre Bernard (Pink Elephant) Contributor

REVIEWERS

OGC would like to recognize the contribution of the following individuals:

Robert Falkowitz, John Groom, Matiss Horodishtiano, Chris Jones, Sue Shaw, Siegfried Schmitt, Dean Taylor and Cheryl Tovizi

and from *it*SMF's International Publications Executive Sub-Committee (IPESC):

Karen Ferris (Lead Assessor), Jorge Aballay (Argentina), Marianna Billington (NZ), Bart van Brabant (Belgium), Jenny Ellwood-Wade (NZ), Ashley Hanna (UK), Sergio Hrabinski (Argentina), Marlon Molina Rodriguez (Spain), David Salischiker (Argentina) and Robert Stroud (US).

1   Introduction

This publication is intended to provide a synopsis of the basic concepts and practice elements of Continual Service Improvement (CSI), which forms part of the core ITIL Service Management Practices. These practices form the ITIL Service Lifecycle on which the concepts of these and all other ITIL Service Management publications are based.

This publication is not intended to replace the ITIL core publications and should not be used in place of the full practice guidance publications. The content in this publication is depicted at a high level and will not be practical as a substitute for the full guidance publication; rather it should serve as a handy quick reference that is portable and helps direct the reader to the full guidance information when needed.

1.1   THE ITIL FRAMEWORK

ITIL Service Management has been practised successfully around the world for more than 20 years. Over this time, the framework has evolved from a specialized set of service management topics with a focus on function to a process-based framework and now to a broader, holistic service lifecycle. The evolution and transformation of ITIL Service Management Practices is the result of the evolution of the IT service management (ITSM) industry itself, through knowledge, experience, technical innovation and thought leadership. The ITIL Service Lifecycle is both a reflection of the industry practice in use today, and concepts that will move us forward in the future of service management philosophies and practices.

The objective of the ITIL Service Management Practices framework is to provide services to business customers that are fit for purpose, stable and which are so reliable that the business views them as a trusted utility.

ITIL Service Management Practices offer best-practice guidance applicable to all types of organizations that provide services to a business. Each publication addresses capabilities having direct impact on a service provider's performance. The structure of the core practice takes form in a service lifecycle. It is iterative and multidimensional. It ensures organizations are set up to leverage capabilities in one area for learning and improvements in others. The core is expected to provide structure, stability and strength to service management capabilities with durable principles, methods and tools. This serves to protect investments and provide the necessary basis for measurement, learning and improvement.

The guidance in the ITIL framework can be adapted for use in various business environments and organizational strategies. The complementary guidance provides flexibility to implement the core in a diverse range of environments. Practitioners can select complementary guidance as needed to provide traction for the core in a given business context, in much the same way as tyres are selected based on the type of automobile, purpose and road conditions. This is to increase the durability and portability of knowledge assets and to protect investments in service management capabilities.

1.2 THE ITIL CORE PRACTICE PUBLICATIONS

The ITIL Service Management Practices comprise three main sets of products and services:

- Core guidance
- Complementary guidance
- Web support services.

1.2.1 ITIL Service Management Practices – core guidance

The core set consists of six publications:

- *The Official Introduction to the ITIL Service Lifecycle*
- *Service Strategy*
- *Service Design*
- *Service Transition*
- *Service Operation*
- *Continual Service Improvement*.

A common structure across all the core guidance publications helps the reader to find references between volumes and to know where to look for similar guidance topics within each stage of the lifecycle.

1.2.2 ITIL Service Management Practices – complementary guidance

This is a living library of publications with guidance specific to industry sectors, organization types, operating models and technology architectures. Each publication supports and enhances the guidance in the ITIL Service Management core. Publications in this category will be continually added to the complementary guidance library and will contain contributions from the expert and user ITSM community. In this way, ITIL Service Management Practices are illustrated in real-life situations and in a variety of contexts that add value and knowledge to your own ITIL practice.

1.2.3 ITIL Service Management Practices – web support services

These products are online, interactive services, which will develop over time and include elements such as the glossary of terms and definitions, the interactive service model, online subscriber services, case studies, templates and ITIL Live® – an interactive expert knowledge centre where users can access time with ITSM experts to discuss questions and issues, and seek advice.

Readers of this key element guide are encouraged to explore the entire portfolio of ITIL Service Management publications and services.

1.3 WHAT IS A SERVICE?

Service management is more than just a set of capabilities. It is also a professional practice supported by an extensive body of knowledge, experience and skills. A global community of individuals and organizations in the public and private sectors fosters its growth and maturity. Formal schemes exist for the education, training and certification of practising organizations, and individuals influence its quality. Industry best practices, academic research and formal standards contribute to its intellectual capital and draw from it.

> **Definition of a service**
> A service is a means of delivering value to customers by facilitating outcomes customers want to achieve without the ownership of specific costs and risks.

1.4 WHAT IS A LIFECYCLE?

The service lifecycle contains five elements, each of which relies on service principles, processes, roles and performance measures. The ITIL Service Lifecycle uses a hub and spoke design, with Service Strategy at the hub, and Service Design, Transition and Operation as the revolving lifecycle stages, anchored by Continual Service Improvement (Figure 1.1). Each part of the lifecycle exerts influence on the others and relies on the others for inputs and feedback. In this way, a constant set of checks and balances throughout the service lifecycle ensures that as business demand changes with business need, the services can adapt and respond effectively to them.

Figure 1.1 The ITIL Service Lifecycle

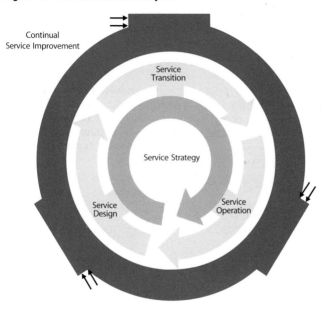

At the heart of the service lifecycle is the key principle – all services must provide measurable value to business objectives and outcomes. ITIL Service Management focuses on business value as its prime objective. Each practice revolves around ensuring that everything a service provider does to manage IT services for the business customer can be measured and quantified in terms of business value. This has become extremely important of late as IT organizations are required to operate as businesses in order to demonstrate a clear return on investment, equating service performance with business value to the customer.

2   The ITIL Service Management Model

The ITIL Service Lifecycle uses models to refine and customize an organization's use of the ITIL Service Management Practices. These models are intended to be reusable in a variety of organizational contexts and to help take advantage of economies of scale and efficiencies.

Central to these models are the overarching process elements that interact throughout the lifecycle and bring power and wisdom to service practices. These service model process elements consist of two main types – lifecycle governance and lifecycle operations. These are depicted in Figure 2.1.

Figure 2.1 Process elements of the ITIL Service Lifecycle

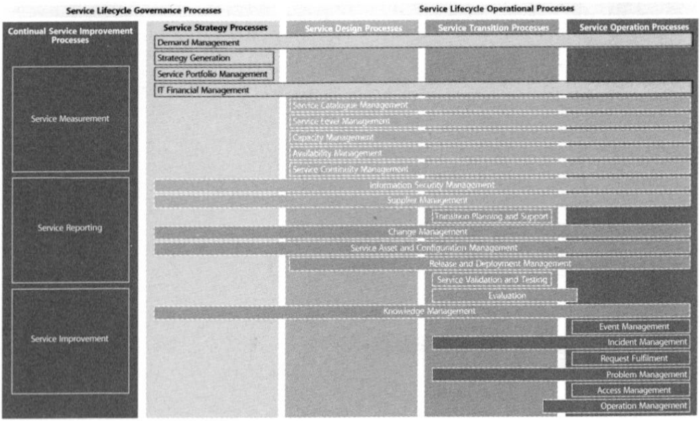

While these processes are non-linear, they do have a logical and sometimes sequential flow. To illustrate this, Figure 2.2 shows the high-level, basic flow of lifecycle process elements in the ITIL Service Lifecycle.

Figure 2.2 A high-level view of the ITIL Service Management Model

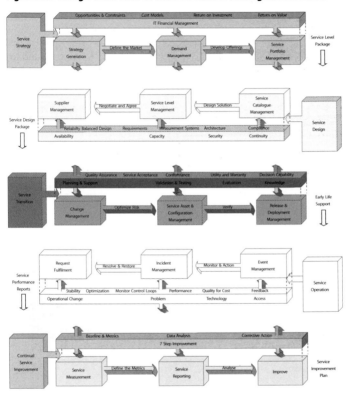

This publication deals with the high-level concepts drawn from the Continual Service Improvement stage of the service lifecycle.

3 Principles of Continual Service Improvement

The primary purpose of Continual Service Improvement (CSI) is continually to align and re-align IT services to the changing business needs by identifying and implementing improvements to IT services that support business processes. These improvement activities support the lifecycle approach through Service Strategy, Service Design, Service Transition and Service Operation. In effect, CSI is about looking for ways to improve process effectiveness and efficiency as well as cost effectiveness. As Figure 3.1 shows, there are many opportunities for CSI.

Consider the following statements about measurements and management:

- You cannot manage what you cannot control
- You cannot control what you cannot measure
- You cannot measure what you cannot define.

Figure 3.1 Continual Service Improvement Model

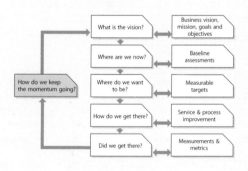

3.1 OBJECTIVES

- Review, analyse and make recommendations on improvement opportunities in each lifecycle phase: Service Strategy, Service Design, Service Transition and Service Operation
- Review and analyse Service Level achievement results
- Identify and implement individual activities to improve IT service quality and improve the efficiency and effectiveness of enabling ITSM processes
- Improve cost effectiveness of delivering IT services without sacrificing customer satisfaction
- Ensure applicable quality management methods are used to support continual improvement activities.

3.2 SCOPE

There are three main areas that CSI focuses on:

- The overall health of ITSM as a discipline
- The continual alignment of the portfolio of IT services with the current and future business needs
- The maturity of the enabling IT processes for each service in a continual service lifecycle model.

To implement CSI successfully, it is important to understand the different activities that can be applied to CSI. The following activities support a continual process improvement plan:

- Reviewing management information and trends to ensure that services are meeting agreed service levels
- Reviewing management information and trends to ensure that the output of the enabling ITSM processes is achieving the desired results
- Periodically conducting maturity assessments against the process activities and roles associated with the process activities to demonstrate areas of improvement or, conversely, areas of concern

- Periodically conducting internal audits verifying employee and process compliance
- Reviewing existing deliverables for relevance
- Making ad-hoc recommendations for approval
- Conducting periodic customer satisfaction surveys
- Conducting external and internal service reviews to identify CSI opportunities and constraints.

3.3 SERVICE IMPROVEMENT

3.3.1 The Deming Cycle

W. Edwards Deming is best known for his management philosophy leading to higher quality, increased productivity and a more competitive position. As part of this philosophy, he formulated 14 points of attention for managers. Some of these points are more appropriate to service management than others. For quality improvement, he proposed the Deming Cycle or Circle. This cycle is particularly applicable in CSI. The four key stages of the Deming Cycle are:

- Plan
- Do
- Check
- Act

after which, a phase of consolidation prevents the circle from rolling back down the hill.

Our goal in using the Deming Cycle is steady, ongoing improvement. It is a fundamental tenet of CSI.

Figure 3.2 shows the Deming Cycle.

Figure 3.2 The Deming Quality Cycle

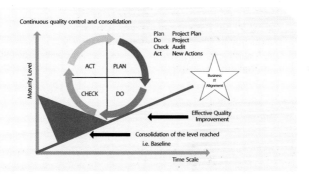

The Deming Cycle is critical at two points in CSI: implementation of CSIs, and for the application of CSI to services and service management processes. At implementation, all four stages of the Deming Cycle are used. With ongoing improvement, CSI draws on the check and act stages to monitor, measure, review and implement initiatives.

The cycle is underpinned by a process-led approach to management where defined processes are in place, the activities are measured for compliance to expected values, and outputs are audited to validate and improve the process (Figure 3.3).

Figure 3.3 The Deming Cycle – adapted for CSI

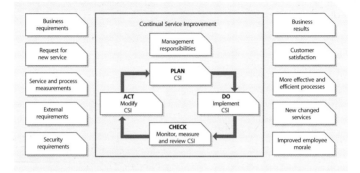

3.3.2 Planning

Planning for improvement initiatives ('Plan') – the planning process should address the following items:

- Scope of CSI
- Establishing goals for improvement including gap analysis, definition of action steps to close any gaps and establishing and implementing measures to assure that the gaps have been closed and benefits achieved
- Objectives and requirements for CSI
- Interfaces between CSI and the rest of the service lifecycle
- Process activities to be developed
- Framework of management roles and responsibilities
- Tools, as appropriate, to support the processes
- Methods and techniques to measure, assess, analyse and report on the quality, effectiveness and efficiency of services and service management processes.

3.3.3 Execution

Implementation of improvement initiative ('Do') – implementing CSI includes the following:

- Funding and budgets required to support CSI
- Documenting roles and responsibilities
- Allocation of roles and responsibilities to work on CSI initiatives
- Documenting and maintaining CSI policies, plans and procedures
- Communicating and training on documented policies, plans and procedures
- Ensuring monitoring, analysis, trend evaluating and reporting tools are in place
- Integrating with Service Strategy, Service Design, Service Transition and Service Operation
- Development and implementation of a project to close the identified gaps, implementation of the improvement to service management processes, and establishing the smooth operation of the process.

3.3.4 Evaluation

Monitor, measure and review services and service management processes ('Check'):

- During this stage, the implemented improvements are compared to the measures of success established in the 'Plan' phase. The comparison determines if a gap still exists between the improvement objectives and the operational process state. Gaps do not necessarily require closure. A gap may be considered tolerable if the actual performance is within allowable limits of performance.

  At the 'Check' stage, the expected output is recommendations for improvement. For example, recommendations to update or modify the Service Catalogue, measurements to be tracked in Service Level Agreements (SLAs), Operating Level Agreements (OLAs) and Underpinning Contracts (UCs) could also come out of this stage.

3.3.5 Act

Continual service and service management process improvement ('Act'):

■ This stage requires implementing the actual service and service management process improvements. A decision to keep the status quo, close the gap or add necessary resources needs to be made to determine if further work is required to close remaining gaps and to allocate resources necessary to support another round of improvement. Project decisions at this stage are the input for the next round of the Plan–Do–Check–Act cycle, closing the loop as input to the next 'Plan' stage.

When applying CSI against services and the service management process, the last two stages of 'Check' and 'Act' play a significant role; however, there are still activities that take place in the 'Plan' and 'Do' stages of the Deming Cycle.

4 Practice of Continual Service Improvement

4.1 BUILDING A SERVICE MEASUREMENT FRAMEWORK

Setting up a framework is as much an art as a science. It may prove difficult at first but the results over time are worth the effort. An organization may go through some trial and error in the beginning so it should not be afraid to admit mistakes on particular measures or targets and make adjustments to the framework.

Keep in mind that service measurement is not an end in itself. The end result should be to improve services and also improve accountability.

One of the first steps in developing a service measurement framework is to understand the business processes and to identify those that are most critical to the delivery of value to the business. The IT goals and objectives must support the business goals and objectives. There also needs to be a strong link between the operational, tactical and strategic level goals and objectives, otherwise an organization will find itself measuring and reporting on performance that may not add any value.

Service measurement is not only looking at the past but also the future – what do we need to be able to do and how can we do things better? The output of any service measurement framework should allow individuals to make operational, tactical or strategic decisions.

Building a service measurement framework means deciding which of the following need to be monitored and measured:

- Services
- Components
- Service Management processes that support the services
- Activities within the process
- Outputs.

Selecting a combination of measures is important to provide an accurate and balanced perspective. The measurement framework as a whole should be balanced and unbiased, and able to withstand change, i.e. the measures are still applicable (or available) after a change has been made.

Whether measuring one or multiple services, the following steps are key to service measurement.

Origins:

- ■ Defining what success looks like – what are we trying to achieve and how will we know when we've achieved it?

Building the framework and choosing measures:

- ■ What do we need to measure that will provide us with useful information that allows us to make strategic, tactical and/or operational decisions?
- ■ What measures will provide us with the data and information we need?
- ■ Setting targets for all measures – this may be set by SLAs or service level targets/objectives that have been agreed internally within IT.

Defining the procedures and policies:

- ■ Define the procedures for making the measurements and determine the tools to be used to support gathering of the data and other measurement activities.
- ■ Identify the roles and responsibilities for service measurement – who will do what?
- ■ Define any policies necessary to support service measurement.
- ■ Decide the criteria for continual improvement initiatives.
- ■ Consider when targets should be raised?

4.1.1 Critical elements of a service measurement framework

For a successful service measurement framework, the following critical elements are required.

A performance framework that is:

- Integrated into business planning
- Focused on business and IT goals and objectives
- Cost effective
- Balanced in its approach on what is measured
- Able to withstand change.

Performance measures that:

- Are accurate and reliable
- Are well defined, specific and clear
- Are relevant to meeting the objectives
- Do not create a negative behaviour
- Lead to improvement opportunities.

Performance targets that:

- Are SMART (specific, measurable, achievable, relevant and time-bound).

Defined roles and responsibilities:

- Who defines the measures and targets?
- Who monitors and measures?
- Who gathers the data?
- Who processes and analyses the data?
- Who prepares the reports?
- Who presents the reports?

4.2 KEY ELEMENTS

4.2.1 Organizational change

Improving service management is to embark upon an organizational change programme. Many organizational change programmes fail to achieve the desired results. Successful ITSM requires understanding the way in which work is done and putting in place a programme of change within the IT organization. This type of change is, by its very nature, prone to difficulties. It involves people and the way they work. People generally do not like to change; the benefits must be explained to everyone to gain their support and to ensure that they break out of old working practices.

Project management structures and frameworks fail to take into account the softer aspects involved in organizational change such as resistance to change, gaining commitment, empowering, motivating, involving and communicating. Experience reveals that it is precisely these aspects that prevent many CSI programmes from realizing their intended aims. The success of a CSI programme is dependant on the buy-in of all stakeholders. Gaining their support from the outset, and keeping it, will ensure their participation in the development process and acceptance of the solution. The first five steps in Figure 4.1 identify the basic leadership actions required.

Figure 4.1 Eight main reasons why transformation efforts fail

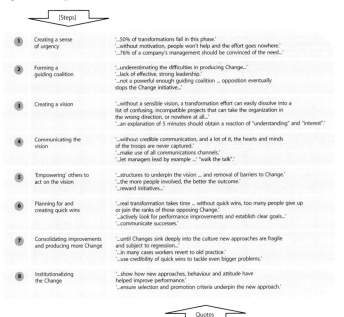

Those responsible for managing and steering the CSI programme should consciously address these softer issues. Using an approach such as John P. Kotter's *Eight Steps to Transforming your Organization*, coupled with formalized project management skills and practices, will significantly increase the chance of success.

Kotter, Professor of Leadership at Harvard Business School, investigated more than 100 companies involved in, or having attempted, a complex change programme and identified 'Eight main reasons why transformation efforts fail'. The main eight reasons, which are shown in Figure 4.1, apply equally to ITSM implementation programmes.

4.2.2 Ownership

The principle of ownership is fundamental to any improvement strategy. CSI is a best practice and one of the keys to successful implementation is to ensure that a specific manager, a CSI manager, is responsible for ensuring the best practice is adopted and sustained throughout the organization. The CSI manager becomes the CSI owner and chief advocate. The CSI owner is accountable for the success of CSI in the organization. This ownership responsibility extends beyond ensuring the CSI practices are embedded in the organization but also to ensuring there are adequate resources (including people and technology) to support and enable CSI. Also included are ongoing CSI activities such as monitoring, analysing, evaluating trends and reporting as well as project-based service improvement activities – activities that are fundamental to the ITIL framework. Without clear and unambiguous accountability, there will be no improvement.

4.2.3 Knowledge Management

Knowledge Management plays a key role in CSI. Within each service lifecycle phase, data should be captured to enable knowledge gain and an understanding of what is actually happening, thus enabling wisdom. This is often referred to as the data–information–knowledge–wisdom (DIKW) model (see Figure 4.2). All too often, an organization will capture the appropriate data, but fail to process the data into information, synthesize the information into knowledge and then combine that knowledge with others to bring us wisdom. Wisdom will lead us to better decisions around improvement.

Figure 4.2 Knowledge Management leads to better IT decisions

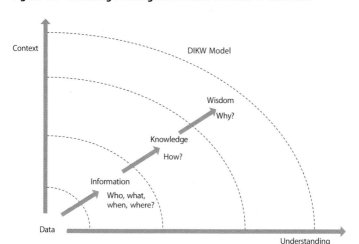

This applies both when looking at the IT services themselves and when drilling down into each individual IT process. Knowledge Management is a mainstay of any improvement process.

'Those who do not learn from history are condemned to repeat it.'

Knowledge Management concepts

Effective Knowledge Management enables a company to optimize the benefits of these changes, while at the same time:

■ Enhancing the **organization's effectiveness** through better decision making enabled by having the right information at the right time, and facilitating enterprise learning through the exchange and development of ideas and individuals

■ Enhancing **customer–supplier relationships** through sharing information and services to expand capabilities through collaborative efforts

■ Improving **business processes** through sharing lessons learned, results and best practices across the organization.

Knowledge Management is key to the overall viability of the enterprise, from capturing the competitive advantage in an industry to decreasing cycle time and cost of an IT implementation. The approach to cultivating knowledge depends heavily on the make-up of the existing knowledge base, and Knowledge Management norms for cultural interaction.

There are two main components to successful Knowledge Management:

■ An **open culture** – knowledge, both best practices and lessons learned, is shared across the organization and individuals are rewarded for it. Many cultures foster an environment where 'knowledge is power' (the more you know that others do not, the more valuable you are to the company). This type of knowledge hoarding is a dangerous behaviour for a company to reward since that knowledge may leave the company at any time. Another tenet of an open culture is a willingness to learn. This is an environment where growing an individual's knowledge base is rewarded and facilitated through open support and opportunities.

■ The **infrastructure** – a culture may be open to knowledge sharing, but without the means or infrastructure to support it, even the best intentions can be impaired, and over time this serves as a demotivator, quelling the behaviour. This infrastructure can be defined in various ways; it may be a technical application or system that allows individuals to conduct online, self-paced training, or it may be a process, such as post-mortems or knowledge sharing activities, designed to bring people together to discuss best practices or lessons learned.

The identification of knowledge gaps and resulting sharing and development of that knowledge must be built into CSI throughout the

IT lifecycle. This also raises the issues of dependencies and priorities. The IT lifecycle itself drives a natural priority of knowledge development and sharing. But, regardless of the IT project's lifecycle stage, it is important to identify and develop the necessary knowledge base prior to the moment where the knowledge may be applied. This may seem obvious and yet the majority of organizations fail to recognize the need to train the individuals until the process is halted due to a skills shortage. Knowledge sharing is an activity that should be fostered prior to, during and after the application of knowledge to the task.

Knowledge Management could be seen at the opposite end of a spectrum from fully automated processes that have all the required knowledge built into the process itself. Service management processes fall somewhere between these two extremes, with the operational processes nearer to the automation of processes than the tactical or strategic processes. This should be taken into account when designing the ITSM processes. Knowledge Management may very well enable quick wins on the more Knowledge Management intensive processes. This is not to imply that there would be a difference of levels of knowledge required for the people participating to the processes – rather that, in order to further develop Service Level Management (SLM) and vendor-management processes, the tactical knowledge needs to be harvested. It is easier to automate the operational level processes than the tactical or strategic processes, which require a greater breadth and depth of knowledge.

Throughout a CSI initiative, a lot of experience and information is acquired. It is important that this knowledge be gathered, organized and accessible. To ensure the ongoing success of the programme, Knowledge Management techniques must be applied. The *Continual Service Improvement* core publication contains detailed information on these.

4.2.4 Governance

Governance has been around the IT arena for decades. The mainframe had significant controls built around its day-to-day operations. With the advent of distributed processing in the early 1990s, then n-tier processing, the Internet, and increasing virtualization, governance and controls lost the strong focus they once had in favour of technologies that were thought to address this. We know, in hindsight, that this was not the case. With the exposure of high-level corporate fraud in the early years of this century, IT was thrust, without warning, into a completely unfamiliar game with incredibly high stakes. Governance is back with a vengeance. IT is now forced to comply with sweeping legislation and an ever-increasing number of external regulations. External auditors are commonplace in large IT shops. IT can no longer mask their operations behind a veil of secrecy or a cloud of obfuscation, but rather they must run an organization that prides itself on its transparency. The core lifecycle publications contain guidance about governance and refer readers to other industry publications that deal directly with governance methods and practices.

4.3   ROLES AND RESPONSIBILITIES

It is important to identify and differentiate between two basic role groupings within CSI: production vs. project. Production roles focus on CSI as a way of life within an organization. These are permanent roles that deal with ongoing service improvement efforts. Typical roles are CSI Manager, Service Manager, Service Owner, Process Owner, Operations Analyst, Measurement Analyst, Reporting Analyst and Quality Assurance Analyst among many others. These roles can range from having responsibility for the day-to-day operations of the IT infrastructure through to defining strategies, designing and transitioning new or changed services to the production environment. Project roles reflect the more traditional approach to improvement efforts based on formal programmes and projects. Taking a leadership position in the creation and adoption of processes and services, this group includes roles such as Executive Sponsor, Process Owners, Process design/implementation/re-engineering team members, Process Adviser and Project Manager among others.

Table 4.1 lists those key activities that require clearly defined roles and responsibilities.

Table 4.1 Key activities and roles assigned

Key activities	Key roles
Collect data and analyse trends compared to baselines, targets, SLAs and benchmarks. This would include output from services and service management processes	CSI Manager, Service Manager, Service Owner, IT Process Owner
Set targets for improvement in efficiency and cost effectiveness throughout the entire service lifecycle	CSI Manager, Service Manager
Set targets for improvements in service quality and resource utilization	CSI Manager, Service Manager, Service Owner, Business Process Owner
Consider new business and security requirements	CSI Manager, Service Manager, Business Process Owner
Consider new external drivers such as regulatory requirements	CSI Manager, Service Manager, Business Process Owner
Create a plan and implement improvements	CSI Manager, Service Manager, Service Owner, Process Owner
Provide a means for staff members to recommend improvement opportunities	CSI Manager, Service Manager
Measure, report and communicate on service improvement initiatives	CSI Manager, Service Manager
Revise policies, processes, procedures and plans where necessary	CSI Manager, Service Manager
Ensure that all approved actions are completed and that they achieve the desired results	CSI Manager, Service Manager, Business Manager, IT Process Owner, Business Process Owner

4.3.1 Roles and responsibilities that support CSI

CSI activities will be successful if specific roles and responsibilities are properly identified. As with many roles, these may or may not be full-time positions; however, it is important that roles are identified at the outset of any CSI initiative. If things change along the way, the roles can be redefined and responsibilities reallocated.

Service Manager

Service Manager is an important role that manages the development, implementation, evaluation and on-going management of new and existing products and services. Responsibilities include business strategy development, competitive market assessment/benchmarking, financial and internal customer analysis, vendor management, inventory management, internal supplier management, cost management, delivery and full lifecycle management of products and/or services. Service Managers are responsible for managing very complex projects in order to achieve objectives and strategies and strive for global leadership in the marketplace. In order to attain this goal, they must evaluate new market opportunities, operating models, technologies and the emerging needs of customers in a company with international scope.

At this level, Service Managers are recognized as global product/service experts. They drive the decision-making processes, manage product/service objectives and strategies, hold internal and external suppliers accountable via formal agreements and provide the integration of individual product plans and new technologies into seamless customer-focused services. Service Managers may also be required to coach other managers (Service Owners, Process Owners) with differing levels of expertise for managing a business function or a particular product/service, within a specified product/service family.

Key responsibilities:

- Provide leadership on the development of the Business Case and product-line strategy and architecture, new service deployment and lifecycle management schedules
- Perform service cost management activities in close partnership with other organizations such as operations, engineering and finance. Many of these organizations are held to strict internal supplier agreements
- Manage various and sometimes conflicting objectives in order to achieve the organization's goals and financial commitments
- Instil a market focus
- Create an imaginative organization that encourages high performance and innovative contributions from its members within a rapidly changing environment.

Service Managers are able to effectively communicate product/service-line strategies to corporate business leaders, and develop partnerships with other organizations within the company with both similar and dissimilar objectives and also with suppliers in order to satisfy internal and external customer needs. This is most often achieved via formalized agreement for both internal and external suppliers.

They must be able to formulate development programmes in response to new market opportunities, assess the impact of new technologies and guide creation of innovative solutions in order to bring best-in-breed solutions to their internal and external customers. They market the development and implementation of products/services that incorporate new technologies or system development. This requires extensive cross-organization communications. They also are able to identify, develop and implement financial improvement opportunities in order to meet the firm's commitments.

Key skills and competencies:

- Previous product/market management experience
- Working knowledge of market analysis techniques and marketing programmes

- Advanced degree or equivalent experience
- Working knowledge of the domestic and international marketplace including industry applications, needs/trends, competitive vendor offerings, outsourcing, licensing, vendor management and customer relationships
- Product knowledge must include complex engineering, telecommunications and data protocols, as well as data processing applications and the ability to analyse the impact of new technologies
- Demonstrated sustained performance in previous assignments
- Sound business judgement
- Negotiating skills
- Human Resources (HR) management skills
- Excellent communications skills
- Accept challenges and manage risk effectively and innovatively
- Produce solutions on time within cost objectives.

CSI Manager

This new role is essential for a successful CSI practice. The CSI Manager is ultimately responsible for the success of all improvement activities. This single point of accountability coupled with competence and authority is essential to a successful improvement programme.

Key responsibilities:

- Responsible for development of the CSI domain
- Responsible for communicating the vision of CSI across the IT organization
- Ensures that CSI roles have been filled
- Works with the Service Owner to identify and prioritize improvement opportunities
- Works with the Service Level Manager to ensure that monitoring requirements are defined
- Works with the Service Level Manager to identify service improvement plans

- Ensures that monitoring tools are in place to gather data
- Ensures that baseline data is captured to measure improvement against it
- Defines and reports on CSI Critical Success Factors (CSFs), key performance indicators (KPIs) and activity metrics
- Identifies other frameworks, models and standards that will support CSI activities
- Ensures that Knowledge Management is an integral part of the day-to-day operations
- Ensures that CSI activities are coordinated throughout the service lifecycle
- Reviews analysed data
- Presents recommendations to senior management for improvement
- Helps prioritize improvement opportunities
- Leads, manages and delivers cross-functional and cross-divisional improvement projects
- Builds effective relationships with the business and IT senior managers
- Identifies and delivers process improvements in critical business areas across manufacturing and relevant divisions
- Sets direction and provides framework through which improvement objectives can be delivered
- Coaches, mentors and supports fellow service improvement professionals
- Possesses the ability to influence positively all levels of management to ensure that service improvement activities are receiving the necessary support and are resourced sufficiently to implement solutions.

Service Owner

The Service Owner is accountable for a specific service within an organization regardless of where the underpinning technology components, processes or professional capabilities reside. Service ownership is as critical to service management as establishing ownership for processes that cross multiple departments.

Key responsibilities:

- Service Owner for a specified service
- Provides input in service attributes such as performance, availability etc.
- Represents the service across the organization
- Understands the service (components, etc.)
- Is the point of escalation (notification) for major Incidents
- Represents the service in Change Advisory Board meetings
- Provides input in CSI
- Participates in internal service review meetings (within IT)
- Works with the CSI Manager to identify and prioritize service improvement
- Participates in external service review meetings (with the business)
- Is responsible for ensuring that the service entry in the Service Catalogue is accurate and is maintained
- Participates in negotiating SLAs and OLAs.

To ensure that a service is managed with a business focus, the definition of a single point of accountability is absolutely essential to provide the level of attention and focus required for its delivery.

The Service Owner is responsible for continual improvement and the management of change affecting the services under their care. The Service Owner is a primary stakeholder in all of the underlying IT processes that enable or support the service they own. For example:

- **Incident Management** – is involved in or perhaps chairs the crisis management team for high-priority Incidents impacting the service owned
- **Problem Management** – plays a major role in establishing the root cause and proposed permanent fix for the service being evaluated
- **Release and Deployment Management** – is a key stakeholder in determining whether a new release affecting a service in production is ready for promotion

- **Change Management** – participates in Change Advisory Board decisions, approving changes to the services they own
- **Asset and Configuration Management** – ensures that all groups which maintain the data and relationships for the service architecture they are responsible for have done so with the level of integrity required
- **Service Level Management** – acts as the single point of contact for a specific service and ensures that the Service Portfolio and Service Catalogue are accurate in relationship to their service
- **Availability and Capacity Management** – reviews technical monitoring data from a domain perspective to ensure that the needs of the overall service are being met
- **IT Service Continuity Management (ITSCM)** – understands and is responsible for ensuring that all elements required to restore their service are known and in place in the event of a crisis
- **IT Financial Management** – assists in defining and tracking the cost models in relationship to how their service is costed and recovered.

Process Owner

The initial planning phase of any ITIL initiative must include establishing the role of Process Owner. This key role is accountable for the overall quality of the process and oversees the management of, and organizational compliance to, the process flows, procedures, data models, policies and technologies associated with the IT service management practices.

The Process Owner performs the essential role of process champion, design lead, advocate, coach and protector. Typically, a Process Owner should be a senior level manager with credibility, influence and authority across the various areas impacted by the activities of the process. The Process Owner is required to have the ability to influence and ensure compliance to the policies and procedures put in place across the cultural and departmental areas of the IT organization.

Reporting Analyst

The Reporting Analyst is a key role for CSI and will often work in concert with the Service Level Management roles. The Reporting Analyst reviews and analyses data from components, systems and sub-systems in order to obtain a true end-to-end service achievement. The Reporting Analyst will also identify trends, and establish if the trends are positive or negative. This information is then used in the presenting of the data.

Key responsibilities:

- Participates in CSI meetings and Service Level Management meetings to ensure the validity of the reporting metrics, notification thresholds and overall solution
- Responsible for consolidating data from multiple sources
- Responsible for producing trends and provides feedback on the trends such as whether the trends are positive or negative, what their impact is likely to be, and if the trends are predictable for the future
- Responsible for producing reports on service or system performance based on the negotiated OLAs, SLAs and improvement initiatives.

Key skills and competencies:

- Good understanding of statistical and analytical principles and processes
- Strong technical foundation in the reporting tool(s)
- Good communication skills
- Good technical understanding and an ability to translate technical requirements and specifications into easily understood reporting requirements.

4.3.2 CSI activities and skills required

Figure 4.3 defines key activities and skills that support CSI activities.

Figure 4.3 Activities and skill levels needed for CSI

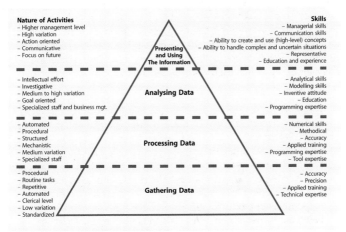

4.4 SERVICE PERFORMANCE

4.4.1 Objective

For all sizes of businesses, private and public organizations, educational institutions, consumers and the individuals working within these organizations, IT services have become an integral means for conducting business. Without IT services many organizations would not be able to deliver the products and services in today's market. As reliance on these IT services increase so do the expectations for availability, reliability and stability. This is why having the business and IT integrated is so important. No longer can they be thought of separately. The same holds true when measuring IT services. It is no longer sufficient to measure and report against the performance of an individual component such as a server or application. IT must now be able to measure and report against an end-to-end service.

For services, there are three basic measurements that most organizations utilize; the *Service Design* publication covers these measures in more detail:

- Availability of the service
- Reliability of the service
- Performance of the service.

Service measurement is really about providing a meaningful view of the IT service as the customer experiences the service. The server may be up, but because the network is down, the customer is not able to connect to the server. Therefore, the IT service was not available even though one or more of the components used to provide the service was available the whole time. Being able to measure against a service is directly linked to the components, systems and applications that are being monitored and reported on.

Measuring at the component level is necessary and valuable, but service measurement must go further than the component level. Service measurement will require someone to take the individual measurements and combine them to provide a view of the true customer experience. Too often, we provide a report against a component, system or application, but do not provide the true service level as experienced by the customer. Figure 4.4 shows how it is possible to measure and report against different levels of systems and components to provide a true service measurement. Even though the figure references availability measuring and reporting, the same can apply for performance measuring and reporting.

Figure 4.4 Availability reporting

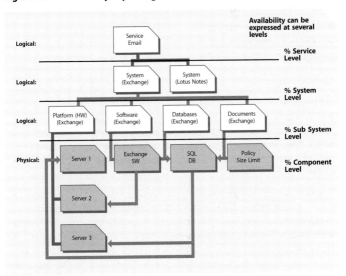

4.4.2 Setting targets

Targets set by management are quantified objectives to be attained.
They express the aims of the service or process at any level and provide
the basis for the identification of problems and early progress towards
solutions and improvement opportunities.

Service measurement targets are often defined in response to business
requirements or they may result from new policy or regulatory
requirements. Service Level Management, through SLAs, will often drive
the target that is required. Unfortunately, many organizations have
had targets set with no clear understanding of the IT organization's
capability to meet the target. That is why it is important that Service Level

Management not only looks at the business requirements, but also the IT capability to meet business requirements.

When first setting targets against a new service, it may be advisable to consider a phased target approach. In other words, the target in the first quarter may be lower than the second quarter. With a new service, it would be unwise to enter into an SLA until overall capabilities are clearly identified. Even with the best Service Design and Transition, no one ever knows how a service will perform until it is actually in production.

Setting targets is just as important as selecting the right measures. It is important that targets are realistic but challenging. Good targets will be SMART (specific, measurable, achievable, relevant and timely). Targets should be clear, unambiguous and easy to understand by those who will be working toward them.

4.5 METRICS – REQUIREMENTS AND VALUE ALIGNMENT

4.5.1 Defining what to measure

Effective service measures concentrate on a few vital, meaningful indicators that are economical, quantitative and usable for the desired results. If there are too many measures, organizations may become too intent on measurement and lose focus on improving results. A guiding principle is to measure that which matters most.

IT has never lacked in the measuring area. In fact, many IT organizations measure far too many things that have little or no value. There is often no thought or effort given to alignment measures to the business and IT goals and objectives. There is often no measurement framework to guide the organization in the area of service measurement. Defining what to measure is important to ensure that the proper measures are in place to support the following:

- **Service performance against the strategic business and IT plans** – this could be a part of a Balanced Scorecard or IT scorecard
- **Risk and compliance with regulations and security requirements for the service** – monitoring of security Incidents and embedding security requirements in the Service Design and Transition practices
- **Business contribution, including, but not limited to, financials** – how does IT support the business in delivering services. As an example, if your organization is an insurance company, the major business services are writing policies and paying claims. Does IT make it easier to write policies and process claims for their agents especially when agents work remotely, such as during times of natural disaster?
- **Key IT processes that support the service** – how do availability, capacity and IT service continuity support the service?
- **Internal and external customer satisfaction** – measuring customer satisfaction to ensure that the customer's needs are being met.

4.5.2 Creating scorecards and reports

Service measurement information will be used for three main purposes: to report on the service to interested parties; to compare against targets; and also to identify improvement opportunities. Reports must be appropriate and useful for all those who use them.

There are typically three distinct audiences for reporting purposes:

- **The business** – is it really focused on delivery to time and budget?
- **IT management** – management will be interested in the tactical and strategic results that support the business.
- **IT operational/technical managers** – these people will be concerned with the tactical and operational metrics that support better planning, coordination and scheduling of resources. The operational managers will be interested in their technology domain measurements such as component availability and performance.

Many organizations make the mistake of creating and distributing the same report to everyone. This does not provide value for everyone.

Creating scorecards that align to strategies

Reports and scorecards should be linked to overall strategy and goals. Using a Balanced Scorecard approach is one way to manage this alignment.

Figure 4.5 illustrates how the overall goals and objectives can be used to derive the measurements and metrics required to support the overall goals and objectives. The arrows point both ways because the strategy, goals and objectives will drive the identification of required KPIs and measurements, but it is also important to remember that the measures are input in KPIs and the KPIs support the goals in the Balanced Scorecard.

It is important to select the right measures and targets to be able to answer the ultimate question of whether the goals are being achieved and the overall strategy supported.

Figure 4.5 Deriving measurements and metrics from goals and objectives

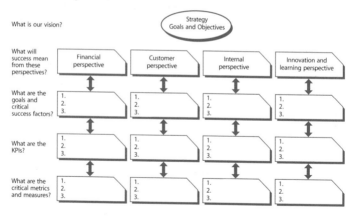

Creating reports

When creating reports, it is important to know their purpose and the details that are required. Reports can be used to provide information for a single month, or a comparison of the current month with other months to provide a trend for a certain time period. Reports can show whether service levels are being met or breached.

Before starting the design of any report, it is also important to know the following:

- ■ Who is the target audience of the report?
- ■ What will the report be used for?
- ■ Who is responsible for creating the report?
- ■ How will the report be created?
- ■ How frequently is the report to be created?
- ■ What information will be produced, shared or exchanged?

One of the first items to consider is who the target audience is. Most senior managers do not want a report that is 50 pages long. They like to have a short summary report and access to supporting details if they are interested. Table 4.2 provides a suitable overview that will fit the needs of most senior managers. This report should be no longer than two pages, or, ideally, a single page if that is achievable without sacrificing readability.

It is also important to know what report format the audience prefers. Some people like text reports, some like charts and graphs with lots of colour, and some like a combination. Be careful about the type of charts and graphs that are used. They must be understandable and not open to different interpretations.

Many reporting tools today produce canned reports but these may not meet everyone's business requirements for reporting purposes. It is wise to ensure that a selected reporting tool has flexibility for creating different reports, that it will be linked to or support the goals and objectives, that its purpose is clearly defined, and that its target audience is identified.

Table 4.2 Example of a summary report format

Report for the month of:	
Monthly overview	This is a summary of the service measurement for the month and discusses any trends over the past few months. This section can also provide input into …
Results	This section outlines the key results for the month.
What led to the results	Are there any issues/activities that contributed to the results for this month?
Actions to take	What action have you taken or would like to take to correct any undesirable results? Major deficiencies may require CSI involvement and the creation of a service improvement plan.
Predicting the future	Define what you think the future results will be.

Reports can be set up to show the following:

- **Results for a service** – supporting reports would be the individual measurements on components
- **Health of a service management process** – this report will have certain process KPI results
- **Functional reports** – such as telephony reports for the Service Desk.

4.6 CSI PROCESS ELEMENTS

4.6.1 The 7-Step Improvement Process

It is obvious that all the activities of the improvement process will assist CSI in some way. It is relatively simple to identify what takes place but the difficulty lies in understanding exactly how this will happen. The improvement process spans not only the management organization but also the entire service lifecycle. This is a cornerstone of CSI.

Figure 4.6 The 7-Step Improvement Process

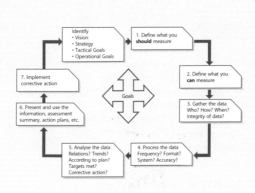

Step One – Define what you should measure

At the onset of the service lifecycle, Service Strategy and Service Design should have identified this information. CSI can then start its cycle all over again at 'Where are we now?'. This identifies the ideal situation for both the business and IT.

Compile a list of what you should measure. This will often be driven by business requirements. Do not try to cover every single eventuality or possible metric in the world. Make it simple. The number of metrics and measurements can grow quite rapidly.

Identify and link the following items:

- Corporate vision, mission, goals and objectives
- IT vision, mission, goals and objectives
- Critical success factors
- Service level targets
- Job description for IT staffs.

Inputs:

- Service Level Requirements and targets
- Service Catalogue
- Vision and mission statements
- Corporate, divisional and departmental goals and objectives
- Legislative requirements
- Governance requirements
- Budget cycle
- Balanced Scorecard.

Step Two – Define what you can measure

This is the CSI activity of 'Where do we want to be?'. By identifying the new service level requirements of the business, the IT capabilities (identified through Service Design and implemented via Service Transition) and the available budgets, CSI can conduct a gap analysis to identify the opportunities for improvement as well as answering the question 'How will we get there?'.

Every organization may find that they have limitations on what can actually be measured. If you cannot measure something, then it should not appear in an SLA.

Start by identifying what you currently are measuring and what additional capabilities you have for measuring. This may be based on the tools you currently have in place. These tools will include service management tools, monitoring tools, reporting tools, investigation tools and others. Compile a list of what each tool can currently measure without any configuration or

customization. Stay away from customizing the tools as much a
configuring them is acceptable.

Perform a gap analysis between what you should measure and wh.
can measure. Report this information back to the business, the custo ners
and IT management. It is possible that new tools are required or that
configuration or customization is required to be able to measure what is
required.

Inputs:

- List of what you should measure
- Process flows
- Procedures
- Work instructions
- Technical and user manuals from existing tools
- Existing reports.

Step Three – Gathering the data

In order to properly answer the 'Did we get there?' question, data must
first be gathered (usually through Service Operations). Data is gathered
based on goals and objectives identified. At this point, the data is raw and
no conclusions are drawn.

Gathering data requires having some form of monitoring in place.
Monitoring could be executed using technology such as application,
system and component monitoring tools or even be a manual process for
certain tasks.

Quality is the key objective of monitoring for CSI. Monitoring will therefore
focus on the effectiveness of a service, process, tool, organization or
Configuration Item (CI). The emphasis is not on assuring real-time service
performance; rather it is on identifying where improvements can be
made to the existing level of service, or IT performance. Monitoring for
CSI will therefore tend to focus on detecting exceptions and resolutions.
For example, CSI is not as interested in whether an Incident was resolved,

⌐ut whether it was resolved within the agreed time, and whether future Incidents can be prevented.

This has two main implications:

- Monitoring for CSI will change over time – there may be an interest in monitoring the e-mail service one quarter, and then move on to look at HR systems in the next quarter
- This means that Service Operation and CSI need to build a process that will help them to agree on what areas need to be monitored and for what purpose.

It is important to remember that there are three types of metrics that an organization will need to collect to support CSI activities as well as other process activities. The types of metrics are:

- **Technology metrics** – these metrics are often associated with component and application-based metrics such as performance, availability, etc.
- **Process metrics** – these metrics are captured in the form of CSFs, KPIs and activity metrics for the service management processes. These metrics can help determine the overall health of a process. Four key questions that KPIs can help answer are around quality, performance, value and compliance in following the process. CSI uses these metrics as input in identifying improvement opportunities for each process.
- **Service metrics** – these metrics are the results of the end-to-end service. Component/technology metrics are used to compute the service metrics.

Service monitoring allows weak areas to be identified, so that remedial action can be taken (if there is a justifiable Business Case), thus improving future service quality. Service monitoring also can show where customer actions are causing the fault and thus lead to identifying where working efficiency and/or training can be improved.

Service monitoring should also address both internal and external suppliers since their performance must be evaluated and managed as well.

Service management monitoring helps determine the health and welfare of service management processes in the following manner:

- **Process compliance** – are the processes being followed? Process compliance seeks to monitor the compliance of the IT organization to the new or modified service management processes and also the use of the authorized service management tool that was implemented.
- **Quality** – how well are the processes working? Monitor the individual or key activities as they relate to the objectives of the end-to-end process.
- **Performance** – how fast or slow? Monitor the process efficiency such as throughput or cycle times.
- **Value** – is this making a difference? Monitor the effectiveness and perceived value of the process to the stakeholders and the IT staff executing the process activities.

Monitoring is often associated with automated monitoring of infrastructure components for performance such as availability or capacity, but monitoring should also be used for monitoring staff behaviour such as adherence to process activities, use of authorized tools as well as project schedules and budgets.

Step Four – Processing the data

Here the data is processed in alignment with the CSFs and KPIs specified. This means that timeframes are coordinated, unaligned data is rationalized and made consistent, and gaps in the data are identified. The simple goal of this step is to process data from multiple disparate sources into an 'apples to apples' comparison. Once we have rationalized the data, we can then begin analysis.

Once data is gathered, the next step is to process the data into the required format. Report-generating technologies are typically used at this stage as various amounts of data are condensed into information for use in the analysis activity. The data is also typically put into a format that provides an end-to-end perspective on the overall performance of a service. This activity begins the transformation of raw data into packaged information. Use the information to develop insight into the performance of the service and/or processes. Process the data into information (i.e. create logical groupings) that provides a better means to analyse the data.

The output of logical groupings could be in spreadsheets, reports generated directly from the service management tool suite, system monitoring and reporting tools or telephony tools such as an automatic call distribution (ACD) tool.

Processing the data is an important CSI activity that is often overlooked. While monitoring and collecting data on a single infrastructure component is important, it is also important to understand the component's impact on the larger infrastructure and IT service. Knowing that a server was up 99.99% of the time is one thing, knowing that no one could access the server is another. An example of processing the data is taking the data from monitoring of the individual components such as the mainframe, applications, WAN, LAN, servers, etc. and processing this into a structure of an end-to-end service from the customer's perspective.

Key questions that need to be addressed in the processing-the-data activity are:

- ■ **What is the frequency of processing the data?** This could be hourly, daily, weekly or monthly. When introducing a new service or service management process it is a good idea to monitor and process in shorter intervals than longer intervals. How often analysis and trend investigation activities take place will drive how often the data is processed.
- ■ **What format is required for the output?** This is also driven by how analysis is done and ultimately how the information is used.
- ■ **What tools and systems can be used for processing the data?**
- ■ **How do we evaluate the accuracy of the processed data?**

Inputs to the processing-the-data activity:

- Data collected through monitoring
- Reporting requirements
- SLAs
- OLAs
- Service Catalogue
- List of metrics, KPIs, CSFs, objectives and goals
- Report frequency
- Report template.

Step Five – Analysing the data

Here, the data becomes information as it is analysed to identify service gaps, trends and the impact on business. It is the analysing step that is most often overlooked or forgotten in the rush to present data to management.

Here is a typical example. Your organization's Service Desk has a trend of reduced call volumes consistently over the last four months. Even though this is a trend, you need to ask yourself the question: 'Is this a good trend or a bad trend?' You do not know if the call reduction is because you have reduced the number of recurring errors in the infrastructure by good problem management activities or if the customers feel that the Service Desk does not provide any value and they have started bypassing the Service Desk and going directly to second-level support groups.

This step takes time. It requires concentration, knowledge, skills, experience, etc. One of the major assumptions is that the automated processing, reporting, monitoring tool has actually done the analysis. Too often people simply point at a trend and say: 'Look, numbers have gone up over the last quarter.' However, key questions need to be asked, such as:

- Is this good?
- Is this bad?

- Is this expected?
- Is this in line with targets?

Be sure to also compare against the clearly defined objectives with measurable targets that were set in the Service Design, Transition and Operation lifecycle stages. Confirmation needs to be sought that these objectives and the milestones were reached. If not, have improvement initiatives been implemented? If so, then the CSI activities start again from the gathering data, processing data and analysing data to identify if the desired improvement in service quality has been achieved. At the completion of each significant stage or milestone, a review should be conducted to ensure the objectives have been met. It is possible here to use the Post-Implementation Review (PIR) from the Change Management process. The PIR will include a review of supporting documentation and the general awareness amongst staff of the refined processes or service. A comparison is required of what has been achieved against the original goals.

During the analysis activity, but after the results are compiled and analysis and trend evaluation have occurred, it is recommended that internal meetings be held within IT to review the results and collectively identify improvement opportunities. It is important to have these internal meetings before you begin presenting and using the information that is the next activity of CSI. The result is that IT is a key player in determining how the results and any actions items are presented to the business.

When analysing data, it is important to seek answers to questions such as:

- Are things running according to plan? This could be operations, a project plan, financial plan, availability, capacity or even an IT Service Continuity Management plan.
- Are targets as defined in SLAs or the Service Catalogue being met?
- Are there underlying structural problems that can be identified?
- Are corrective actions required?

- Are there any trends? If so then what are the trends showing? Are they positive trends or negative trends?
- What is leading to or causing the trends?

Reviewing trends over a period of time is another important task. It is not good enough to see a 'snapshot' of a data point at a specific moment in time, but to look at the data points over a period of time. How did we do this month compared to last month, this quarter compared to last quarter, this year compared to last year?

It is not enough to look only at the results – look also at what led to the results for the current period. If we had a bad month, did we have an anomaly that took place? Is this a demonstrable trend or simply a one-off?

Without analysis, the data is merely information. With analysis comes improvement opportunities.

Throughout CSI, assessment should identify whether targets were achieved and, if so, whether new targets (and therefore new KPIs) need to be defined. If targets were achieved but the perception has not improved, then new targets may need to be set and new measures put in place to ensure that these new targets are being met.

When analysing the results from process metrics keep in mind that a process will only be as efficient as its limited bottleneck activity. So, if the analysis shows that a process activity is not efficient and continually creates a bottleneck, then this would be a logical place to begin looking for a process improvement opportunity.

Step Six – Presenting and using the information

Here the answer to 'Did we get there?' is formatted and communicated in whatever way necessary to present to the various stakeholders an accurate picture of the results of the improvement efforts. Knowledge is presented to the business in a form and manner that reflects their needs and assists them in determining the next steps.

The sixth step is to take our knowledge and present it; that is, turn it into wisdom by utilizing reports, monitors, action plans, reviews, evaluations and opportunities. Consider the target audience; make sure that you identify exceptions to the service, benefits that have been revealed, or can be expected. Data gathering occurs at the operational level of an organization. Format this data into knowledge that all levels can appreciate and gain insight into their needs and expectations.

There are usually three distinct audiences:

- **The business** – their real need is to understand whether IT delivered the service they promised at the levels they promised, and, if not, what corrective actions are being implemented to improve the situation
- **Senior (IT) management** – this group is often focused on the results surrounding CSFs and KPIs, such as customer satisfaction, actual vs. plan, and costing and revenue targets. Information provided at this level helps determine strategic and tactical improvements on a larger scale. Senior (IT) management often wants this type of information provided in the form of a Balanced Scorecard or IT scorecard format to see the big picture at one glance.
- **Internal IT** – This group is often interested in KPIs and activity metrics that help them plan, coordinate, schedule and identify incremental improvement opportunities.

Often there is a gap between what IT reports and what is of interest to the business. IT is famous for reporting availability in percentages such as 99.85% available. In most cases, this is not calculated from an end-to-end perspective but only mainframe availability or application availability and often does not take into consideration LAN/WAN, server or desktop downtime. In reality, most people in IT do not know the difference between 99.95% and 99.99% availability let alone the business. Yet reports continue to show availability achievements in percentages. What the business really wants to understand is the number of outages that occurred and the duration of the outages with analysis describing the impact on the business processes; in essence, unavailability expressed in a commonly understood measure: time, which includes when it occurs and for how long.

Step Seven – Implementing corrective action

The knowledge gained is used to optimize, improve and correct services. Managers identify issues and present solutions. The corrective actions that need to be taken to improve the service are communicated and explained to the organization. Following this step, the organization establishes a new baseline and the cycle begins anew.

CSI identifies many opportunities for improvement; however, organizations often cannot afford to implement all of them. Based on goals, objectives and types of service breaches, an organization needs to prioritize improvement activities. Improvement initiatives can also be externally driven by regulatory requirements, changes in competition, or even political decisions.

If organizations were implementing corrective action according to CSI, there would be no need for this publication. Corrective action is often done in reaction to a single event that caused a (severe) outage to part or all of the organization. Other times, the squeaky wheel will get noticed and specific corrective action will be implemented in no relation to the priorities of the organization, thus taking valuable resources away from real emergencies. That is common practice but obviously not best practice.

After a decision to improve a service and/or service management process is made, then the service lifecycle continues. A new Service Strategy may be defined, Service Design builds the changes, Service Transition implements the changes into production and then Service Operation manages the day-to-day operations of the service and/or service management processes. Keep in mind that CSI activities continue through each phase of the service lifecycle.

4.6.2 Service measurement

Complex feedback and control loop

An organization can find improvement opportunities throughout the entire service lifecycle. Figure 4.7 shows the interaction that should take place between each lifecycle phase. An IT organization does not need to wait until a service or service management process is transitioned into the operations area to begin identifying improvement opportunities.

Figure 4.7 CSI and the service lifecycle

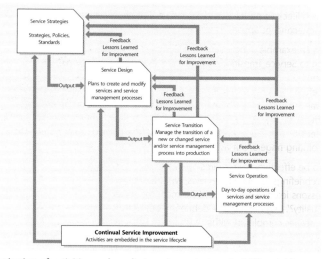

Monitoring of activities and results is an important part of CSI activities. The results or output need to be compared against the norms in order to identify if an improvement opportunity is needed.

CSI will make extensive use of methods and practices found in many ITIL processes such as Problem Management, Availability Management and Capacity Management used throughout the lifecycle of a service. The use of the outputs, in the form of flows, matrices, statistics or analysis reports, will provide valuable insight into the design and operation of services. This information, combined with new business requirements, technology specifications, IT capabilities, budgets, trends and possibly external legislative and regulatory requirements will be vital to CSI to determine what needs to be improved, prioritize it and suggest improvements, if required.

Each lifecycle phase will provide an output to the next lifecycle phase. This same concept applies to CSI.

As an example, a new service is designed or modified and passed on to Service Transition. Service Transition can provide feedback to Service Design on any design issues or that everything is looking good before the service moves into Service Operation. CSI does not have to wait for the service to be implemented and in operation before any improvement opportunities are identified and communicated. These CSI steps throughout the lifecycle should not be viewed as placing blame or pointing fingers, but as a learning tool for improvement.

To be effective, CSI requires open and honest feedback from IT staff. Debriefings, or activity reviews, work well for capturing information about lessons learned such as 'Did we meet the timelines?' and 'Did we provide quality?'. Segmenting the debriefing or review into smaller, individual activities completed within each phase of the service lifecycle and capturing the lessons learned within that phase makes the plethora of data more manageable (Figure 4.8).

Figure 4.8 ITSM Monitor Control Loop

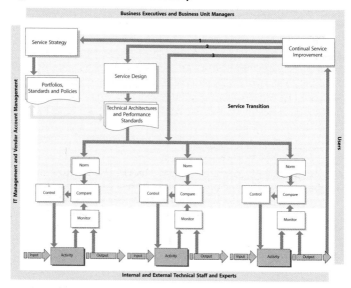

4.6.3 Interpreting and using metrics

Results must be examined in context of the objectives, environment and any external factors. Therefore, after collecting the results, organizations will conduct measurement reviews to determine how well the indicators worked and how the results contribute to objectives.

Metrics can be used for multiple purposes such as to:

■ **Validate** – are we supporting the strategy and vision?
■ **Justify** – do we have the right targets and metrics?

- **Direct** – based on factual data, people can be guided to change behaviour
- **Intervene** – take corrective actions such as identifying improvement opportunities.

Another key use of measurement and metrics is for comparison purposes. Measures by themselves may tell the organization very little unless there is a standard or baseline against which to assess the data. Measuring only one particular characteristic of performance in isolation is meaningless unless it is compared with something else that is relevant. The following comparisons are useful:

- Comparison against the baseline
- Comparison against a target or goal
- Comparison with other organizations – be sure to understand that the strategy, goals and objectives of other organizations may not be in alignment with yours so there may be driving factors in the other organization that you do not have or it could be the other way around
- Comparison over time such as day to day, week to week, month to month, quarter to quarter, or year to year
- Comparison between different business units
- Comparison between different services.

Measures of quality allow for measuring trends and the rate of change over a period of time. Examples could be measuring trends against standards that are set up either internally or externally and could include benchmarks, or it could be measuring trends with standards and targets to be established. This is often done when first setting up baselines.

A minor or short-term deviation from targets should not necessarily lead to an improvement initiative. It is important to set the criteria for the deviations before an improvement programme is initiated.

Comparing and analysing trends against service level targets or an actual SLA is important as it allows for early identification of fluctuations in service delivery or quality. This is important not only for internal service providers, but also when services have been outsourced. It is important to identify any deviations and discuss them with the external service provider in order to avoid any supplier relationship problems. Speed and efficiency of communication when there are missed targets is essential to the continuation of a strong relationship.

Using the measurements and metrics can also help define any external factors that may exist outside the control of the internal or external service provider. The real world needs to be taken into consideration. External factors could include anything from language barriers to governmental decisions.

Individual metrics and measures by themselves may tell an organization very little from a strategic or tactical point of view. Some types of metrics and measures are often more activity based than volume based, but are valuable from an operational perspective. Examples could be:

- Services used
- Mapping of customers to services
- Frequency of use of each service
- Times of day each service is used
- The way each service is used (internally or externally through the web)
- Performance of each component used to provide the service
- Availability of each component used to provide the service.

Each of these measures by themselves will provide some information that is important to IT staff, including the technical managers who are responsible for Availability and Capacity Management, as well as those who may be responsible for a technology domain, such as a server farm, an application or the network, but it is the examination and use of all the measurements and metrics together that delivers the real value. It is important for someone to own the responsibility to not only look at these measurements as a whole, but also to analyse trends and provide interpretation of the meaning of the metrics and measures.

Analysing metrics

Data analysis transforms the information into knowledge of the events that are affecting the organization. More skill and experience is required to perform data analysis than data gathering and processing. Verification against goals and objectives is expected during this activity. This verification validates that objectives are being supported and value is being added. It is not sufficient to simply produce graphs of various types but to document the observations and conclusions.

Once the data is processed into information, you can then analyse the results, looking for answers to questions such as:

- Are there any clear trends?
- Are they positive or negative trends?
- Are changes required?
- Are we operating according to plan?
- Are we meeting targets?
- Are corrective actions required?
- Are there underlying structural problems?
- What is the cost of the service gap?

Here you apply knowledge to your information. Without this, you have nothing more than sets of numbers showing metrics that are meaningless. It is not enough to simply look at this month's figures and accept them without question, even if they meet SLA targets. You should analyse the figures to stay ahead of the game. Without analysis, you merely have information. With analysis, you have knowledge. If you find anomalies or poor results, then look for ways to improve.

4.6.4 Service reporting

The business likes to see a historical representation of the past period's performance that portrays their experience; however, it is more concerned with those historical events that continue to be a threat going forward, and how IT intends to mitigate against such threats.

Cross-referenced data must still be presented which align precisely to any contracted, chargeable elements of the delivery, which may or may not be technical depending upon the business focus and language used within contracts and SLAs.

It is not satisfactory simply to present reports which depict adherence (or otherwise) to SLAs, which in themselves are prone to statistical ambiguity. IT needs to build an actionable approach to reporting, i.e. this is what happened, this is what we did, this is how we will ensure it does not impact you again, and this is how we are working to improve the delivery of IT services generally.

A reporting ethos that focuses on the future as strongly as it focuses on the past also provides the means for IT to market its wares directly aligned to the positive or negative experiences of the business.

An ideal approach to building a business-focused service-reporting framework is to take the time to define and agree the policy and rules with the business and Service Design about how reporting will be implemented and managed.

This includes:

- Targeted audience(s) and the related business views on what the service delivered is
- Agreement on what to measure and what to report on
- Agreed definitions of all terms and boundaries
- Basis of all calculations
- Reporting schedules
- Access to reports and medium to be used
- Meetings scheduled to review and discuss reports.

Right content for the right audience

Simple and effective customizable and automated reporting is crucial to a successful, ongoing reporting system that is seen as adding value to the business. Over time, many of the initial standard reports may become

obsolete in favour of the regular production of custom reports that have
been shaped to meet changing business needs and become the standard.

The end result is the targeted recipient having clear, unambiguous and
relevant information in a language and style they understand and like,
accessible in the medium of their choice, and detailing the delivery of IT
into their environment within their boundaries, without such information
being clouded by the data related to the delivery of IT into other areas of
the business.

Table 4.3 Categories for assessing business performance

Category	Definition
Productivity	Productivity of customers and IT resources
Customer satisfaction	Customer satisfaction and perceived value of IT services
Value chain	Impact of IT on functional goals
Comparative performance	Comparison against internal and external results with respect to business measures or infrastructure components
Business alignment	Criticality of the organization's services, systems and portfolio of applications to business strategy
Investment targeting	Impact of IT investment on business cost structure, revenue structure or investment base
Management vision	Senior management's understanding of the strategic value of IT and ability to provide direction for future action

Business impact

Measure what actions are invoked for any disruption in service that
adversely affects the customer's business operation, processes or its own
customers.

Supplier performance

Whenever an organization has entered into a supplier relationship where some services or parts of services have been outsourced or co-sourced it is important to measure the performance of the supplier. Any supplier relationship should have defined, quantifiable measures and targets; measurement and reporting should be against the delivery of these measures and targets. Besides those discussed above, service measurements should also include any process metrics and KPIs that have been defined.

One of CSI's key sets of activities is to measure, analyse and report on IT services and ITSM results. Measurements will, of course, produce data. This data should be analysed over time to produce a trend. The trend will tell a story that may be good or bad. It is essential that measurements of this kind have ongoing relevance. What was important to know last year may no longer be pertinent this year.

As part of the measuring process, it is important to confirm regularly that the data being collected and collated is still required and that measurements are being adjusted where necessary. This responsibility falls on the owner of each report or dashboard. They are the individuals designated to keep the reports useful and to make sure that effective use is being made of the results.

4.6.5 Assessments and baselines

Assessments

Assessments are the formal mechanisms for comparing the operational process environment to the performance standards for the purpose of measuring improved process capability and/or to identify potential shortcomings that could be addressed. The advantage of assessments is they provide an approach to sample particular elements of a process or the process organization that impact the efficiency and the effectiveness of the process.

The initial step in the assessment process is to choose (or define) the maturity model and in turn the maturity attributes to be measured at each level. A suggested approach is to turn to the best-practice frameworks such as Capability Maturity Model® Integration (CMMI), the Control Objectives for Information and related Technology (COBIT) framework, ISO/IEC 20000 or the process maturity framework. These frameworks define maturity models directly or a model can be inferred. The frameworks are also useful in the definition of process maturity attributes.

What to assess and how

The assessment's scope is one of the key decisions. Scope should be based on the assessment's objective and the expected future use of process assessments and assessment reports. Assessments can be targeted broadly at those processes currently implemented or focused specifically where known problems exist within the current process environment. There are three potential scope levels:

- **Process only** – assess only process attributes based on the general principles and guidelines of the process framework which defines the subject process
- **People, process and technology** – extend the process assessment to include assessment of the skills, roles and talents of the managers and practitioners of the process, as well as the ability of the process-enabling technology deployed to support the objectives and transaction state of the process
- **Full assessment** – extend the people, process and technology assessment to include an assessment of the culture of acceptance within the organization, the ability of the organization to articulate a process strategy, the definition of a vision for the process environment as an 'end state', the structure and function of the process organization, the ability of process governance to assure that process objectives and goals are met, the business/IT alignment via a

process framework, the effectiveness of process reporting/metrics, and the capability and capacity of decision-making practices to improve processes over time.

All these factors are compared to the maturity attributes of the selected maturity model.

Assessments can be conducted by the sponsoring organization or with the aid of a third party. The advantages of conducting a self-assessment is the reduced cost and the intellectual lift associated with learning how to gauge objectively the relative performance and progress of an organization's processes. Of course, the downside is the difficulty associated with remaining objective and impartial during the assessment.

Benchmarking

Benchmarking (also known as 'best-practice benchmarking' or 'process benchmarking') is a process used in management, particularly strategic management, in which organizations evaluate various aspects of their processes in relation to best practice, usually within their own sector. This then allows organizations to develop plans on how to adopt such best practice, usually with the aim of increasing some aspect of performance. Benchmarking may be a one-time event, but is often treated as a continual process through which organizations continually seek to challenge their practices.

Benchmarking is a management technique to improve performance. It is used to compare performance between different organizations – or different units within a single organization – undertaking similar processes. Benchmarking is an ongoing method of measuring and improving products, services and practices against the best that can be identified in any industry anywhere.

Baselines

An important beginning point for highlighting improvement is to establish baselines as markers or starting points for later comparison. Baselines are also used to establish an initial data point to determine if a service or process needs to be improved. As a result, it is important that baselines are documented, recognized and accepted throughout the organization. Baselines must be established at each level: strategic goals and objectives, tactical process maturity, and operational metrics and KPIs.

If a baseline is not initially established, the first measurement efforts will become the baseline. That is why it is essential to collect data at the outset, even if the integrity of the data is in question. It is better to have data to question than to have no data at all. Figure 3.1 defines the improvement model.

Gap analysis

Gap analysis is a business assessment tool enabling an organization to compare where it is currently and where it wants to go in the future. This provides the organization with insight to areas that have room for improvement. This can be used to determine the gap between 'What do we want?' and 'What do we need?', for example.

The process involves determining, documenting and approving the variance between business requirements and current capabilities. Gap analysis naturally flows from benchmarking or other assessments such as service or process maturity assessments. Once the general expectation of performance is understood, then it is possible to compare that expectation with the level of performance at which the company currently functions. This comparison becomes the gap analysis. Such analysis can be performed at the strategic, tactical or operational level of an organization.

Gap analysis can be conducted from different perspectives such as:

- Organization (e.g. HR)
- Business direction
- Business processes
- Information technology.

Gap analysis provides a foundation for how much effort, in terms of time, money and human resources, is required to have a particular goal achieved (e.g. how to bring a service from a maturity level of 2 to 3).

Figure 4.9 and Table 4.4 illustrate the many gaps that can exist between the CSI model and the service lifecycle.

Figure 4.9 Service gap model

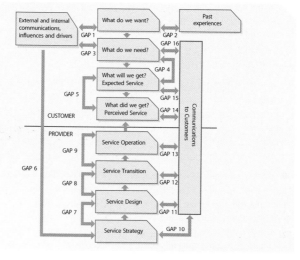

Table 4.4 Explanation of the gaps in the service gap model

Gap	Description
1	This gap comes from the interpretation of the information coming from the outside and how it influences or directs the question 'What do we want?'.
2	This gap comes from the interpretation of past experiences or the lack of data, information and knowledge to properly reduce this gap and how it influences or directs the question 'What do we want?'.

3	This gap comes from the interpretation of the information coming from the outside and the organization's incorrect assessments of what it really needs.
4	This gap comes from the translation of the information into requirements.
5	This gap comes from either a lack of communication or from unclear communication. Often expectations are not set properly or are unrealistic.
6	This gap comes from the interpretation of the information coming from the outside and how it influences or directs the service strategy.
7	This gap comes from the interpretation of Service Strategy into design specifications and from the limitation of the tools used to translate requirements and specifications into a plan.
8	This gap comes from the interpretation of Service Strategy and design specifications and from the limitation of the tools used to create and transition the service into existence.
9	This gap comes from the interpretation of what the provider perceives the deliverables to be and from either a lack of communication or from unclear communication. Often expectations are not set properly or are unrealistic even from the perspective of the provider.
10	This gap comes from the interpretation of what the message should be, what the message is and the frequency of the message.
11	This gap comes from the interpretation of what the message should be, what the message is and the frequency of the message.
12	This gap comes from the interpretation of what the message should be, what the message is and the frequency of the message.
13	This gap comes from the interpretation of what the message should be, what the message is and the frequency of the message.
14	This gap comes from the interpretation of what the message should be, what the message is and the frequency of the message.
15	This gap comes from the interpretation of what the message should be, what the message is and the frequency of the message.
16	This gap comes from the interpretation of what the message should be, what the message is and the frequency of the message.

4.7 CHALLENGES

Every organization will have its unique set of challenges. As with implementing any type of change within an organization, one of the major challenges will be managing the behavioural changes that are required.

The other issue is that CSI often requires adequate tools for monitoring and gathering the data, analysing the data for trends and reporting on the data. CSI does not happen only through automation but also requires resources to be allocated to CSI activities. The resources need to understand their roles and responsibilities and have the correct skill sets to execute the CSI activities.

Listed below are some of the common challenges that you may encounter when implementing CSI:

- Lack of management commitment
- Inadequate resources, budget and time
- Lack of mature service management processes
- Lack of information, monitoring and measurements
- Lack of Knowledge Management
- Resistance to planning and reluctance to be proved wrong
- Lack of corporate objectives, strategies, policies and business direction
- Lack of IT objectives, strategies and policies
- Lack of knowledge and appreciation of business impacts and priorities
- Diverse and disparate technologies and applications
- Resistance to change and cultural change
- Poor relationships, communication and a lack of cooperation between IT and the business
- Lack of tools, standards and skills
- Tools too complex and costly to implement and maintain
- Over-commitment of resources with an associated inability to deliver (e.g. projects always late or over budget)
- Poor supplier management and/or poor supplier performance.

4.8   TECHNOLOGY CONSIDERATIONS

CSI activities will require software tools to support the monitoring and reporting on IT services as well as to underpin the ITSM processes. These tools will be used for data gathering, monitoring, analysis, reporting for services and will also assist in determining the efficiency and effectiveness of IT service management processes. The longer-term benefits to be gained are cost savings and increased productivity, which in turn can lead to an increase in the quality of the IT service provision.

From a service perspective, the use of tools enables an organization to gain the ability to understand the health of its services from an end-to-end perspective. Even if an organization is not able to monitor end-to-end services, it should be able to monitor, identify trends and perform analyses on the key components that make up an IT service.

From a process perspective, the use of tools enables centralization of key processes and automation and integration of core service management processes. The raw data collected in the databases can be analysed resulting in the identification of trends. Preventive measures can then be implemented thereby increasing the stability, reliability and availability of the IT infrastructure.

The ITSM software tools of today have expanded their scope from mere 'point' solutions focusing on the Service Desk or Change Management to complete, fully integrated solution suites. Current tools represent a paradigm shift into the new era of enterprise resource planning (ERP) systems for IT. For decades, IT has provided systems to run the business; now, there are systems to run IT.

4.9   TOOLS TO SUPPORT CSI ACTIVITIES

As part of the assessment of 'Where do we want to be?', the requirements for enhancing tools need to be addressed and documented. These requirements vary depending on both the process and technology maturity. Technology specifically means systems and service management toolsets used for both monitoring and controlling the systems and infrastructure components and for managing process-based workflows, such as Incident Management.

Without question, service management tools are indispensable. However, good people, good process descriptions, and good procedures and working instructions are the basis for successful service management. The need and the sophistication of the tools required depend on the business need for IT services and, to some extent, the size of the organization.

In a very small organization, a simple in-house developed database system may be sufficient for logging and controlling Incidents. However, in large organizations, very sophisticated distributed and integrated service management tools may be required, linking all the processes with systems management toolsets. While tools can be important assets, in today's IT-dependent organizations, they are a means, not an end in themselves. When implementing service management processes, look at the way current processes work. Each organization's unique need for management information should always be its starting point. This will help define the specifications for the tools best suited to that organization.

There are many tools that support the core ITSM processes and others that support IT governance as a whole that will require integration with the ITSM tools. Information from both of these toolsets typically needs to be combined, collated and analysed collectively to provide the overall business intelligence required to effectively improve on the overall IT service provision.

4.10   IMPLEMENTING CONTINUAL SERVICE IMPROVEMENT

This publication has discussed implementing CSI from two perspectives. First and foremost is the implementation of CSI activities around services. Second is the implementation of CSI around service management processes. However, if your organization does not have very mature service management processes then it is usually difficult to execute the 7-Step Improvement Process for services.

Immature processes usually have poor data quality if any at all. This is often due to no processes or very ad hoc processes. Other organizations have multiple processes working with multiple tools being used to support the processes. If any monitoring is going on it may be at a component or application level but not from an end-to-end service perspective. There is no central gathering point for data, no resources allocated to process and analyse the data, and reporting consists of too much data broken into too many segments for anyone to analyse. Some organizations do not have any evidence of reporting at all.

4.10.1 Critical considerations for implementing CSI

Before implementing CSI, it is important to have identified and filled the critical roles that have been identified in Section 4.3. This would include a CSI Manager, Service Owner and reporting analyst. A Service Level Manager is really needed to be the liaison between the business and IT.

Monitoring and reporting on technology metrics, process metrics and service metrics need to be in place.

Internal service review meetings need to be scheduled in order to review from an internal IT perspective the results achieved each month. These internal review meetings should take place before any external review meeting with the business.

4.10.2 Value to the business

Perspectives on benefits

There are four commonly used terms when discussing service improvement outcomes:

- Improvements
- Benefits
- Return on investment (ROI)
- Value on investment (VOI).

Much of the angst and confusion surrounding IT process improvement initiatives can be traced to the misuse of these terms. Below is the proper use:

- **Improvements** – outcomes that when compared to the 'before' state, show a measurable increase in a desirable metric or decrease in an undesirable metric.

  Example: ABC Corp. achieved a 15% reduction in failed changes through implementation of a formal Change Management process.

- **Benefits** – the gains achieved through realization of improvements, usually but not always expressed in monetary terms.

  Example: ABC Corp.'s 15% reduction in failed changes has saved the company £395,000 in productivity and re-work costs in the first year.

- **ROI** – the difference between the benefit (saving) achieved and the amount expended to achieve that benefit, expressed as a percentage. Logically, one would like to spend a little to save a lot.

  Example: ABC Corp. spent £200,000 to establish the formal Change Management process that saved £395,000. The ROI at the end of the first year of operation was therefore £195,000 or 97.5%.

- **VOI** – the extra value created by establishment of benefits that include non-monetary or long-term outcomes. ROI is a subcomponent of VOI.

  Example: ABC Corp.'s establishment of a formal Change Management process (which reduced the number of failed changes) improved the ability of ABC Corp. to respond quickly to changing market conditions and unexpected opportunities resulting in an enhanced market position. In addition, it promoted collaboration between business units and the IT organization and freed up resources to work on other projects that otherwise may not have been completed.

4.10.3 Creating a return on investment

The ROI challenge needs to take into consideration many factors. On one side is the investment cost. This is the money an organization pays to improve services and service management processes. These costs will be internal resource costs, tool costs, consulting costs, etc. It is often easy to come up with these costs.

On the other side is what an organization can gain in a return. These returns are often hard to define. In order to be able to compute these items it is important to know the following:

- **What is the cost of downtime?** This would include both lost productivity of the customers and the loss of revenue.
- **What is the cost of doing rework?** How many failed changes have to be backed out and reworked?
- **What is the cost of doing redundant work?** Many organizations that do not have clear processes in place and good communication often find that redundant work is being done.
- **What is the cost of non-value-added projects?** Many projects have been fully funded and resourced, but, due to changing requirements, no longer add value, but the project moves forward instead of being stopped.
- **What is the cost of late delivery of an application?** Does this impact on the ability to deliver a new service or possibly an additional way to deliver an existing service?
- **What is the cost of escalating Incidents to second- and third-level support groups instead of resolving Incidents at the first level?** There is often a difference in utilization of staff in second-level and third-level support groups. The more we escalate Incidents to these groups, the less time they have to work on projects that they may also be assigned to.
- **What is the fully allocated hourly cost for different employee levels?**

4.11 KEY MESSAGES AND LESSONS

CSI takes a commitment from everyone in IT working throughout the service lifecycle to be successful at improving services and service management processes. It requires ongoing attention, a well-thought-out plan, consistent attention to monitoring, analysing and reporting results with an eye toward improvement. Improvements can be incremental in nature but also require a huge commitment to implement a new service or meet new business requirements.

This guide spelled out the seven steps of the CSI process. All seven steps need attention. There is no reward for taking a short cut or not addressing each step in a sequential nature. If any step is missed, there is a risk of not being efficient and effective in meeting the goals of CSI.

IT services must ensure that proper staffing and tools are identified and implemented to support CSI activities. It is also important to understand the difference between what should be measured and what can be measured. Start small – do not expect to measure everything at once. Understand the organizational capability to gather data and process the data. Be sure to spend time analysing data, as this is where the real value comes in. Without analysis of the data, there is no real opportunity to truly improve services or service management processes. Think through the strategy and plan for reporting and using the data. Reporting is partly a marketing activity. It is important that IT focus on the value added to the organization as well as reporting on issues and achievements. In order for steps five to seven to be carried out correctly, it is imperative that the target audience is considered when packaging the information.

An organization can find improvement opportunities throughout the entire service lifecycle. An IT organization does not need to wait until a service or service management process is transitioned into the operations area to begin identifying improvement opportunities.

5   Further guidance and contact points

Visit www.itil-officialsite.com for more information on all things ITIL.

- Office of Government Commerce (2007) *Service Strategy*, TSO
  ISBN-13: 978-0113310456
- Office of Government Commerce (2007) *Service Design*, TSO
  ISBN-13: 978-0113310470
- Office of Government Commerce (2007) *Service Transition*, TSO
  ISBN-13: 978-0113310487
- Office of Government Commerce (2007) *Service Operation*, TSO
  ISBN-13: 978-0113310463
- Office of Government Commerce (2007) *The Official Introduction to the
  ITIL Service Lifecycle*, TSO
  ISBN-13: 978-0113310616

Visit www.iso.org for more information on:

- ISO/IEC 20000   Information Technology Service Management
- ISO/IEC 27001   Information technology – Security techniques
  Information Security Management Systems
- ISO/IEC 17799   Information technology – Security techniques
  Code of practice for Information Security Management
- ISO/IEC 19770   Information technology – Software asset management
  Part 1: Processes
- ISO/IEC 15504   Information technology – Process assessment.

Visit www.itgi.org for more information on COBIT.

Visit www.isaca.org for more information on IS Audit.

Visit www.sei.cmu.edu/cmmi for more information on CMMI.

Visit www.johnkotter.com for more information on Kotter's 'Eight Steps for Organizational Change':

- John P. Kotter, Holger Rathgeber, Peter Mueller and Spenser Johnson (2006) *Our Iceberg Is Melting: Changing and Succeeding Under Any Conditions*, St Martin's Press

  ISBN-13: 978-0312361983

- John P. Kotter (1999) *What Leaders Really Do*, Harvard Business School Press

  ISBN-13: 978-0875848976

- John P. Kotter (1996) *Leading Change*, Harvard Business School Press

  ISBN-13: 978-0875847474

- John P. Kotter and Dan S. Cohen (2002) *The Heart of Change: Real-Life Stories of How People Change Their Organizations*, Harvard Business School Press

  ISBN-13: 978-1578512546.

Six Sigma – www.ge.com/sixsigma:

- Peter S. Pande, Robert P. Neuman and Roland R. Cavanagh (2000) *The Six Sigma Way: How GE, Motorola, and Other Top Companies are Honing Their Performance*, McGraw-Hill

  ISBN-13: 978-0071358064

- Pete Pande and Larry Holpp (2001) *What Is Six Sigma?*, McGraw-Hill

  ISBN-13: 978-0071381857

LEAN

- Michael L. George (2003) *Lean Six Sigma for Service: How to Use Lean Speed and Six Sigma Quality to Improve Services and Transactions*, McGraw-Hill

  ISBN-13: 978-0071418218.